D0831504

BOOK ANALYSIS

Written by Natalia Torres Behar
Translated by Emma Hanna

The Great Gatsby

BY F. SCOTT FITZGERALD

Bright
≡Summaries.com

F. SCOTT FITZGERALD

AMERICAN WRITER

- **Born in Saint Paul (Minnesota) in 1896.**
- **Died in Hollywood (California) in 1940.**
- **Notable works:**
  - *This Side of Paradise* (1920), novel
  - *The Beautiful and the Damned* (1922), novel
  - *Tender Is the Night* (1934), novel

Francis Scott Key Fitzgerald, better known simply as F. Scott Fitzgerald, was born into an Irish Catholic family just prior to the dawn of the 20th century. He studied at Princeton University, although he never graduated, and later enlisted in the army to fight in the First World War. He went on to become one of the foremost American novelists of the 20th century, whose novels are best known for the way they capture the spirit of the "Roaring Twenties".

His debut novel, *This Side of Paradise* (1920), garnered him enough recognition that he was able to start publishing his short stories in prestigious magazines such as *The Saturday Evening Post*, and he came to be seen as one of the figures who most completely embodied the "American Dream" of the 1920s. He and his wife Zelda Sayre, who was one of the most important people in his life and served as the inspiration for a number of his fictional characters, moved to the French Riviera in 1924. During his time there, he finished writing the novel that is generally considered his masterpiece: *The Great Gatsby* (1925). The novel is set in the Prohibition era, and tells the story of a bootlegger (alcohol smuggler) who creates a false aristocratic identity and uses it to climb to the top of the social ladder, allowing him the freedom to indulge in all kinds of decadence, before fading away to become a ghost in his own mansion as he pours all his money and energy into trying to win the heart of Daisy Buchanan.

Fitzgerald went on to write two more novels: *Tender Is the Night* (1934), which was the last of his novels to be published during his lifetime, and *The Last Tycoon* (1941), which he never completed and was published posthumously. The latter novel is an exploration of the darker side of Hollywood – which Fitzgerald was intimately familiar with, as he worked as an uncredited screenwriter in the years leading up to his death.

THE GREAT GATSBY

THE CRUMBLING OF THE AMERICAN DREAM

- **Genre:** novel
- **Reference edition:** Fitzgerald, F. S. (1992) *The Great Gatsby*. Ware: Wordsworth.
- **1st edition:** 1925
- **Themes:** the past, dreams, symbols, the American Dream, the Roaring Twenties, nostalgia, power, money, love, greed, racism

Fitzgerald's novels are some of the most famous literary chronicles of the 1920s in the USA, and *The Great Gatsby* in particular is seen as one of the most important novels from the "Jazz Age", a period during which American society was more stable and prosperous than ever before (until the Great Depression utterly reversed this situation a few years later). The elation of winning the First World War had yet to dissipate, and the prohibition of the sale and consumption of alcohol provided bootleggers with an opportunity to rake in enormous profits on the margins of society, creating an underground subculture where partying, gambling and having a good time were the only things that mattered. *The Great Gatsby* takes place against this backdrop, and Fitzgerald's characters must constantly fight against their desires for a wild, decadent life, which ultimately reduces their existence to a meaningless struggle to keep up appearances and the hollow pursuit of materialism. In the world of *The Great Gatsby*, this is the reality of the American Dream.

SUMMARY

THE RISE OF JAY GATSBY

The main themes and ideas explored in the novel are closely linked to the way the character of Jay Gatsby develops over the course of the story. However, everything we know about the life and personality of Gatsby is filtered through the perspective of Nick Carraway, the narrator. This greatly influences the reader's understanding of the novel, as we are led to doubt the veracity of the account we are reading on a number of occasions – not necessarily because of the way Nick describes the events in question, but because of his opinions about Gatsby, as he often seems to harbour too much affection towards Gatsby to speak about him objectively.

The very first lines of the novel demonstrate how subjective Nick's point of view is:

> "In my younger and more vulnerable years my father gave me some advice that I've been turning over in my mind ever since.
> 'Whenever you feel like criticising anyone,' he

told me, 'just remember that all the people in this world haven't had the advantages that you've had.'" (p. 3)

Interestingly, the meaning of these opening lines becomes clearer as we read more of the book and become acquainted with Nick and the other characters, including Daisy Buchanan and her aggressive husband Tom. Nick seems to be warning us that it is easy for us to judge these characters, given that they come across as generally unlikeable, although it is unclear whether or not this is his conscious intention.

The novel is set in New York during the 1920s, a time when the sale and consumption of alcohol was banned in the United States. The Buchanans live in East Egg, one of the most fashionable neighbourhoods on Long Island, while Nick lives in West Egg, which is a slightly less glamourous area that lies opposite East Egg. Although both areas are very upmarket, East Egg enjoys a more sophisticated reputation because its inhabitants are mostly from 'old money', rather than the 'new money' individuals who have only recently made their fortune and have proceeded to flock to West Egg.

Jay Gatsby is a very wealthy but mysterious man who lives in an enormous mansion next to Nick's house, and who spends a great deal of time in the evenings in his garden, gazing across the bay at a glowing green light in East Egg .

Gatsby throws wild parties at his home every Saturday night, and everyone is welcome to attend and join the drunken revels. The extreme decadence of these parties, which even feature a live jazz band, stir up every guest's curiosity about the source of Gatsby's wealth, which is also a mystery to the reader in the early chapters of the novel. Gatsby's business dealings seem somewhat shady, as does his claim of having attended Oxford University, and his position in society is always left rather ambiguous. Initially, the reader's only way of getting to know the character of Gatsby is through the extravagant parties he throws, but like many other aspects of the novel – notably including Nick's opinions about Gatsby – these parties serve two contra- dictory functions by simultaneously answering our questions about Gatsby and giving rise to fresh doubts about his life and past.

During one conversation with Jordan Baker, a woman with whom Nick embarks on a relationship, she reveals that Daisy and Gatsby were lovers before he went off to fight in the war and Daisy married Tom. At this point in the novel, Gatsby's main goal is revealed: to find Daisy and win her back. All of his other ideas, aims and beliefs stem from this single, overarching objective, which also serves as a metaphor for the American Dream and is symbolised by the glowing green light at the end of Daisy's dock, which Gatsby is constantly transfixed by. This representation of a complex, abstract concept through a much simpler idea is very characteristic of Fitzgerald's style, particularly in *The Great Gatsby*.

GATSBY'S DOWNFALL

Nick arranges for Gatsby and Daisy to meet, so that they can rekindle their former love affair. Everything seems to be going smoothly, and Gatsby gradually wins back Daisy's heart – and everything she represents to him, namely success, money and class. However, things take a turn for the worse when Gatsby meets Daisy's husband Tom, who starts probing into Gatsby's past and eventually learns the truth about him: that he comes from a poor family and that he owes his fortune to a rich old man called Dan Cody, who taught him all there is to know about smuggling, allowing him to make staggering sums of money by selling alcohol on the black market. As the problems facing Gatsby begin to multiply, the façade of the American Dream begins to crumble, revealing its true face (at least according to the narrator and, by extension, the author). Underneath the superficial glitz and glamour, the American Dream proves empty and meaningless:

> "I thought of Gatsby's wonder when he first picked out the green light at the end of Daisy's dock. He had come a long way to this blue lawn, and his dream must have seemed so close that he could hardly fail to grasp it. He did not know that it was already behind him, somewhere back in that vast obscurity beyond the city." (p. 115)

The most important scene in the novel takes place in a hotel room in the centre of New York. In this scene, Tom and Gatsby argue over who has the "right" to be with Daisy, and it is revealed that Gatsby is a bootlegger. The theme of social class, which runs throughout the novel, is never more apparent than in this scene, as Daisy realises that she cannot bring herself to leave Tom and bring scandal upon herself. However, the novel's most shocking plot twist is yet to come: while Daisy and Gatsby are driving back along Long Island together in Gatsby's car, Tom's lover Myrtle is hit by the car and killed. This is when the characters' true colours are finally revealed: Gatsby, the unmasked charlatan, admits to Nick that Daisy was the one who was driving at the time of the accident, but says that he will take the blame. Meanwhile, Tom seals Gatsby's fate by telling Myrtle's husband George where he can find the man who supposedly killed his wife, and George shoots Gatsby before committing suicide.

Somehow, Gatsby's death does not come as a shock to the reader – after all, what other possible way could this dream have ended? Every element of the story seems to have been crafted to suggest that Gatsby's dream was destined to be shattered: for example, the story is primarily set in the twin locations of East Egg and West Egg, which seem to be in constant conflict with each other. If anything, the fate of Tom and Daisy is the most surprising aspect of the end of the novel, as they simply go back to their old lives and relationship with apparent indifference. Meanwhile, Nick ends his relationship with Jordan and arranges Gatsby's funeral, at which there are almost no guests – not even Daisy – except for Nick and a strange man who turns out to be Gatsby's father, who offers us some insight into Gatsby's childhood, revealing that the wealth he acquired was the fulfilment of a childhood dream. The lack of attendees at the funeral stands in stark contrast to the crowds that used to flock to Gatsby's house for his parties. As the novel draws to a close, Nick stands in the garden, gazing out over the waters of the bay at the green light at the end of Daisy's garden, and mulls over the power of nostalgia and the innate human desire to repeat the past: "So we beat on, boats against the current, borne back ceaselessly into the past" (p. 115).

CHARACTER STUDY

NICK CARRAWAY

Nick is the narrator of the novel. He is from the American Midwest, attended Yale University and fought in the First World War. When the novel begins, he is 29 years old and has just moved to West Egg, where he has rented a small house beside Jay Gatsby's mansion. He turns 30 later in the novel. Because of his optimistic, reserved and tolerant nature, people whose secrets are weighing them down frequently choose to confide in him. As a result, he acts as an intermediary between Gatsby and Daisy, and they rekindle their romance through him. This mirrors the way that the entire narrative is filtered through his occasionally sarcastic thoughts and perceptions.

JAY GATSBY

The character of Jay Gatsby was allegedly based on the real-life figure of Max von Gerlach, who moved in the same New York social circles as

Fitzgerald and turned to bootlegging to make his fortune after serving in the First World War. In any case, Gatsby is a young millionaire from North Dakota who lives in a Gothic mansion in West Egg and is notorious for throwing astonishingly extravagant parties every Saturday night. However, no one knows where he comes from or how he made his fortune. This secrecy is deliberate, as the source of his wealth is later revealed to be his involvement in the illicit trafficking of alcohol during Prohibition. He is obsessed with Daisy Buchanan, whom he met during his days as an officer in the First World War. After the war ended, he briefly studied at Trinity College, Oxford. His story is gradually revealed as Nick grows closer to him and earns his trust. Nick's opinion of Gatsby is inherently contradictory, as he considers him to be dishonest, tasteless and utterly unprincipled when it comes to money, but he also harbours deep admiration for him because of his ability to make his dreams a reality. This quality is what makes Gatsby "great".

DAISY BUCHANAN (NÉE FAY)

The character of Daisy was partly based on Fitzgerald's wife, Zelda. She is an attractive young woman from an aristocratic family, and she has therefore grown up surrounded by the luxuries of high society. Nick Carraway is her second cousin.

Despite her privileged position, Daisy is plagued by doubts and uncertainty: although she is married, she feels drawn to Gatsby, with whom she had a relationship before he went overseas to fight in the First World War. She promised to wait for him, but eventually broke this promise in 1919 by marrying Tom Buchanan, a young man from a wealthy aristocratic family. The novel largely hinges on her conflicting desires for Gatsby and Tom. Since 1919, Gatsby has poured all of his energy into his quest to win Daisy back – his obsession with her was even the reason why he originally got involved with criminal activities in order to make his fortune. Gatsby idealises her because of her grace, sophistication and social standing, and has coveted these qualities since he first met her in North Dakota. As such, winning Daisy back has become his ultimate dream and goal in life.

Although Gatsby's image of Daisy is not necessarily incorrect, Nick notes that it is at least incomplete, because it discounts the less pleasant aspects of her personality, as she is also shallow, capricious and indifferent; in fact, her speech about her newborn daughter tells us a lot about her own personality: "I'm glad it's a girl. And I hope she'll be a fool – that's the best thing a girl can be in this world, a beautiful little fool" (p. 13). Nick describes her as someone who does not truly care about anything, and who thinks that money can solve any problem life throws at her, as proven when she eventually chooses Tom over Gatsby, and her superficial nature is frequently alluded to:

> "Sometimes she and Miss Baker talked at once, unobtrusively and with a bantering inconsequence that was never quite chatter, that was as cool as their white dresses and their impersonal eyes in the absence of all desire." (p. 10)

TOM BUCHANAN

Tom is Daisy's husband. He is from an aristocratic family and is very wealthy, which has made him extremely arrogant. Through Nick's eyes, he is shown to be racist and sexist, and he cannot accept Daisy's infidelity with Gatsby, even though he has been having an extramarital affair of his own with Myrtle; he even plans a confrontation over it. He cannot abide failure, and cannot bear it when things do not go his way. Accordingly, it seems that things eventually turn out the way he wants them to in the novel, as Daisy ends up choosing the advantages of money and class that he can offer her, even after Gatsby gives her a second chance at life by taking the fall for her when she causes the accident that kills Myrtle.

JORDAN BAKER

Jordan is a friend of Daisy, and starts a relationship with Nick. She is very competitive and selfish, and represents some of the women of the 1920s who, despite not actively fighting for equal rights for women, tried to act like men. In other words, they sought to access the privileges that the misogynistic world they lived in usually reserved for men, without doing anything to tear these oppressive patriarchal structures down. She is described as beautiful and is an accomplished liar who can bend the truth to suit her own purposes.

MYRTLE WILSON

Myrtle is Tom's lover, and her husband owns a garage in the "valley of ashes". Nick says that there is "an immediately perceptible vitality about her" (p. 18), and she is fiercely determined to improve her social standing. However, Tom treats her as nothing more than an object.

GEORGE WILSON

George is Myrtle's husband and loves her deeply, so he is left devastated when he discovers that she has been having an affair. His years of owning a garage have left him world-weary, and he spirals into despair when Myrtle is killed. He bears certain similarities to Gatsby and to Fitzgerald himself, as all three of them poured everything they had into romances which eventually led to their doom.

MEYER WOLFSHEIM

Meyer Wolfsheim is a friend of Gatsby and is a high-ranking figure in the world of organised crime. He helped Gatsby to make his fortune during Prohibition, and his continued contact with Gatsby suggests that they may both still be involved in illicit dealings.

ANALYSIS

FORM

Structure

The Great Gatsby is a short novel which comprises nine chapters, and charts the rise and fall of the titular character, Jay Gatsby, which is a metaphor for the way the American Dream crumbled into dust in the 1920s. Most of the novel is set in two locations which are established at the start of the novel: West Egg and East Egg. These two neighbourhoods and the contrasting ideas, values and qualities they represent are in constant conflict throughout the novel.

The main conflict in the novel revolves around the fortune Gatsby has illegally amassed as part of his futile quest to win back Daisy's affections. However, he is unable to truly escape his mysterious past, and in the end Daisy always chooses Tom (and the upper-class social circle he represents, which Gatsby desperately wishes to be part of), first by marrying him instead of waiting for Gatsby, then by going back to him after her affair with Gatsby. The crux of this narrative thread can be found in Chapters 5 and 6, in which Daisy and Gatsby are reunited, and it comes to a head in Chapter 7, in which Tom confronts Gatsby in a room at the Plaza Hotel. By setting such a crucial scene in this opulent location, Fitzgerald is able to paint a portrait of the main concerns that shaped American society in the 1920s, namely the endemic superficiality, decadence and taste for luxury that swept through the nation during that decade.

Style and language

Gatsby is prepared to do anything in his power to win Daisy back, which is a metaphor for the lengths people were prepared to go to in order to attain the American Dream. However, Gatsby is also shown to idealise Daisy, which is emphasised through the writing style by the incorporation of some elegant flourishes in terms of its construction, even though Fitzgerald's style is generally realistic and direct. Similarly, the prose never gets bogged down in complex rhetoric, even though Fitzgerald addresses a number of weighty themes in his analysis of the major issues that faced society during the 1920s. On the contrary, he cleverly employs specific metaphors to convey and explore much more complex concepts – though this is not to say that the metaphors themselves are simplistic or lacking in complexity.

Similarly, Nick's narration is always somewhat ambiguous in nature, and can even be contra-dictory on occasion: while he seems to condemn Gatsby's actions, decadence and lack of a moral compass at certain times, there are a number of passages in the novel in which he expresses his considerable admiration for the bootlegger. These passages tend to echo and emphasise Nick's esteem for Gatsby by employing a more nostalgic tone.

Geography

In *The Great Gatsby*, various geographical areas are used to personify different aspects of North American society in the 1920s. For example, New York is portrayed as a city which is utterly devoid of morals and inhibitions, where cynicism and vice reign supreme and the population's only concerns are seeking pleasure and wealth at any price and by any means necessary. By contrast, rural areas such as Minnesota are depicted as bastions of traditional values which harbour nothing but scorn for the 'new money' generation, whose only aim is to become rich and powerful as quickly as possible. Finally, the novel juxtaposes two distinct regions of New York: the self-made millionaires of West Egg flaunt their wealth and decadence, while the conservative aristocrats of East Egg waste away in the rigid confines of their superficial, hollow lives.

THEMES

The American Dream

The Great Gatsby is a profound examination of the Roaring Twenties in the United States, and one of the most interesting aspects of the novel is its use of specific metaphors to illustrate the way the idea of the American Dream began to crumble over the course of this decade. As the novel follows Gatsby's obsessive quest to win back Daisy's affection, it also explores the defining features of an era shaped by decadence and unprecedented prosperity through a cast of characters who leap at any excuse for a lavish party, and whose thirst for power, money and instant gratification is insatiable.

Fitzgerald uses two seemingly opposing perspectives to examine the theme of the destruction of the American Dream: the members of the established aristocracy, who reside in East Egg, and the brash social climbers of West Egg, such as Gatsby, who have ostensibly achieved the American Dream by making their own fortune. Even though the aristocracy was traditionally viewed as inherently superior, being from 'old money' is shown to be no more desirable than making your own fortune and joining the ranks of the 'new money', as the characters from an aristocratic background are portrayed as vapid, shallow and cruel. Conversely, Gatsby's defining qualities are shown to be positive, namely loyalty and protectiveness towards the people he cares about (even if they are not from the same social class as him). This protectiveness drives him to wait patiently opposite Daisy's house until 4 o'clock in the morning to make sure that Tom is not mistreating her (Chapter 8).

However, Fitzgerald does not oversimplify things, and uses these qualities to give his characters complexity and depth: for example, Gatsby's good heart eventually leads to his death, as he refuses to let Daisy take responsibility for the accident in which Myrtle was killed, and plans to claim that it was his fault instead. In some ways, it could be said that the members of the two opposing social classes represented in the novel each possess qualities that the other side lacks, but rather than complementing each other, they prove mutually destructive – and the American Dream, symbolised by Gatsby, is one of the casualties in this conflict.

Weather

The novel's tone and narrative are frequently personified or complemented by the weather. This creates the impression that every element of the novel is working together in harmony, and that the universe is conspiring to ensure that events occur in one particular way, rather than in any other. Instead of simply adding to the atmosphere of the novel, these descriptions of the weather act as clues which reveal something to the reader. For example, when Gatsby is murdered by Wilson, he is swimming in his pool on the first day of autumn, despite the strong breeze that is blowing. In literature, wind is often used as a symbol of change, and the reader can therefore intuit that Gatsby's fortunes are about to be irrevocably reversed.

Symbolism

The Great Gatsby features a number of recurring motifs which can be interpreted as symbols that represent more abstract ideas or concepts. Although these possible readings are merely subjective interpretations of these objects' potential meanings and should not be considered definitive, they allow the reader to gain greater insight into Fitzgerald's portrayal of the 1920s.

One excellent example of these symbols is the green light at the end of the dock in Daisy's garden. Starting in the very first chapter of the novel, Gatsby uses this light as a kind of guide through the darkness. This light could therefore have two possible symbolic meanings: firstly, it could be a semi-literal representation of Gatsby's quest to find Daisy and win her back. Alternatively, it could be a more metaphorical symbol of the desire to achieve the American Dream.

The valley of ashes located between West Egg and New York City could be interpreted as a metaphor for the hollowness and waste that resulted from the decadence and unrestrained pleasure-seeking that characterised the Jazz Age. However, it could also be interpreted as social commentary on the vast gulf between this dissolute lifestyle that the wealthy were able to indulge in, and the poverty that the poorer citizens in society are forced to endure, as embodied by George Wilson, whose life among the ashes seems to have drained him of vitality.

The valley of ashes is also home to the eyes of Doctor T. J. Eckleburg: an old timeworn billboard which features an enormous pair of blue eyes behind a pair of glasses. Although these eyes could be interpreted as a metaphor for God, Fitzgerald seems to suggest that the objects and symbols in the novel can only have meaning conferred on them by the characters themselves. In other words, the connection between these eyes and God only exists in the mind of George Wilson. These symbols would be utterly meaningless if the novel's complex characters did not constantly see metaphors in the world around them; instead, they would seem like mere descriptive flourishes which are devoid of any real importance. However, the power granted to the characters through their ability to confer meaning on these objects could also be seen as a covert nod to the reader and the role they play in reading the novel, as their understanding of the novel completes and redefines its meaning. This idea is explored to a certain degree in Chapter 8, when Nick imagines Gatsby's final thoughts before his death through a series of images and symbols.

Jazz

Jazz plays a very important role in the novel, as it not only evokes the atmosphere of New York in the 1920s, but also acts as a metaphor for the idle, decadent lives of the wealthy upper classes. Jazz became very popular in New York, and later variants of the genre were heavily influenced by the big bands which dominated popular music during that era. This stylised, universal, extravagant style of music perfectly complements the aesthetic of the novel, the characters it portrays and the themes it explores. For example, while Daisy does not seem to be an extravagant person at first glance, she always allows her decisions to be primarily influenced by the issues of money, pleasure and power, and she does not think about the potential consequences her actions could have for others (as seen when Gatsby dies in an attempt to protect her and she does not even attend his funeral, and instead simply moves on as if nothing had happened).

FURTHER REFLECTION

SOME QUESTIONS TO THINK ABOUT...

- From Nick's perspective, what makes Gatsby so "great"?
- What kind of narrator is Nick? Is his version of events always reliable?
- According to the novel, what role do symbols play in our lives?
- How are the concepts of dreams, happiness and time related to the idea of the American Dream and North America as a whole within the novel?
- How are the locations in the novel linked to the characters' values and personalities?
- Compare the characters of Gatsby and Tom. How are they similar and how are they different?
- How are women viewed and what role do they play in the novel?

- How could the scene depicting Gatsby's funeral be interpreted? Why do you think no one attended his funeral even though his parties were so popular?

We want to hear from you!
Leave a comment on your online library
and share your favourite books on social media!

FURTHER READING

REFERENCE EDITION

- Fitzgerald, F. S. (1992) *The Great Gatsby*. Ware: Wordsworth.

REFERENCE STUDIES

- Barbarese, J. T. (1992) "The Great Gatsby" and the American Dream. *The Sewanee Review*. 100(4), pp. cxxi-cxxiv.
- Bryer, J. R. and VanArsdale, N. P., eds. (2009) *Approaches to Teaching Fitzgerald's* The Great Gatsby. New York: The Modern Language Association of America.
- Ellis, J. (1972) The 'Stoddard Lectures' in *The Great Gatsby*. American Literature. 44(3), pp. 470-471.
- Meehan, A. (2014) Repetition, Race, and Desire in *The Great Gatsby. Journal of Modern Literature*. 37(2), pp. 76-91.

RECOMMENDED READING

- Bloom, H., ed. (2003) *F. Scott Fitzgerald's* The Great Gatsby. New York: Chelsea House Publishers.

- Bruccoli, M. J., ed. (1985) *New Essays on* The Great Gatsby. New York: Cambridge University Press.

- Lehan, R. D. (1969) *F. Scott Fitzgerald and the Craft of Fiction*. Carbondale, Illinois: Southern Illinois University Press.

- Turnbull, A. (1962) Scott Fitzgerald. New York: Charles Scribner's Sons.

ADAPTATIONS

- *The Great Gatsby*. (1974) [Film]. Jack Clayton. Dir. USA: Paramount.

- *The Great Gatsby*. (2000) [Film]. Robert Markowitz. USA: Granada Entertainment.

- *The Great Gatsby*. (2013) [Film]. Baz Luhrmann. Dir. USA: Warner Bros.

www.brightsummaries.com

Ebook EAN: 9782808001960

Paperback EAN: 9782808001977

Legal Deposit: D/2017/12603/619

Cover: © Primento

Digital conception by Primento, the digital partner of
publishers.